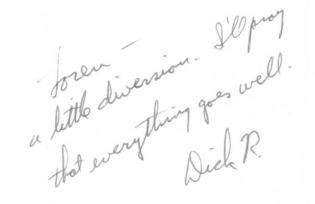

Loren —
a little diversion. I'll pray
that everything goes well.
Dick R.

ALL YOU CAN EAT

OTHER BOOKS BY S. GROSS

How Gross

I Am Blind and My Dog Is Dead

An Elephant Is Soft and Mushy

More Gross

Why Are Your Papers in Order?

Dogs Dogs Dogs

Cats Cats Cats

Grateful acknowledgment is made to *The New Yorker* for permission to reprint cartoons which, as indicated throughout this book, originally appeared in that magazine.

FIRST EDITION

Designer: Kim Llewellyn

Library of Congress Cataloging-in-Publication Data

All you can eat.

1. Food habits—Caricatures and cartoons.   2. American wit and humor, Pictorial.   I. Gross, S. (Sam)
NC1426.A44   1987   741.5′973   87-45054
ISBN 0-06-015807-7

---

87   88   89   90   91   HOR   10   9   8   7   6   5   4   3   2   1

ALL YOU CAN EAT

a feast of great food cartoons

edited by S. Gross

O'Neill

HARPER & ROW, PUBLISHERS, New York
Cambridge, Philadelphia, San Francisco, Washington
London, Mexico City, São Paulo, Singapore, Sydney

1817

AARON BACALL

"It's going to be great!
All natural ingredients."

"Let's just go in and see what happens."

LOU MYERS

"How nouvelle is your cuisine?"

PETER PORGES

BORIS DRUCKER

"I like New York because there's a world-famous
restaurant opening every day."

SIDNEY HARRIS

"This looks good. The first ingredient
is whole wheat flour."

L. TREPEL

"They ran out of hog dogs, so I got you
a tofu burger with sprouts."

LIZA DONNELLY

© 1978 The New Yorker Magazine, Inc.

LEE LORENZ

"Welcome to 'Bagel World.'"

S.GROSS

SAM GROSS

"Five blocks of quiche places
and not one shoe repair."

DAVID PASCAL

"There you are . . . eggs Benedict"

PETER PORGES

MARTY MURPHY

"I could never hold a job as a chef 'cause
I burned the food and put too much spice in it.
Then—voila—along comes the Cajun craze."

SIDNEY HARRIS

". . . recalling Sun Glo orange juice, Corn-X
cereal and Lift coffee . . ."

MARTY MURPHY

"Sorry . . . sir . . . rules . . . are . . . rules. . . . No . . . tie . . . no . . . service."

CATHERINE O'NEILL

"Angst. Weltschmerz. And now, my God,
Wiener schnitzel!"

JOHN CALLAHAN

"I never realized you knew how to use
chopsticks!"

ELDON DEDINI

ELI BAUER

MIKE TWOHY

"Explain to me the giant cookie phenomenon."

OLDDEN

DICK OLDDEN

EDWARD KOREN

© 1985 The New Yorker Magazine, Ine.

"Kate, this is the wonderful man I told you about who has such
a strong hand with garlic and fresh thyme."

WARREN MILLER

SGROSS

SAM GROSS

"This is where Edgar goes for his
power luncheons."

BILL MAUL

"Hi! I'm Marv and this is my partner, Ol' Blue.
We'll be eating your leftovers tonight."

CHARLES SAUERS
© 1984 The New Yorker Magazine, Inc.

"Everything that was bad for you is now good for you."

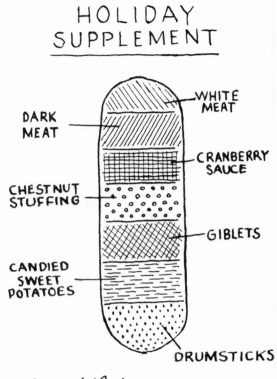

HOLIDAY SUPPLEMENT

WHITE MEAT

DARK MEAT

CRANBERRY SAUCE

CHESTNUT STUFFING

GIBLETS

CANDIED SWEET POTATOES

DRUMSTICKS

Stuart Leeds

STUART LEEDS
© 1984 The New Yorker Magazine, Inc.

BRIAN SAVAGE

Where Are They Now?

The kiwi-hotshot of the '70s.

Love ya - Kiwi

Now living outside the spotlight in Elmview, New Hampshire.

Souvenirs of the past lie tucked away in the attic.

KIWI magazine

I ♥ KIWIS

KIWI IN SONG

Perhaps, someday, the grandchildren will be interested.

R. Chast
ROZ CHAST

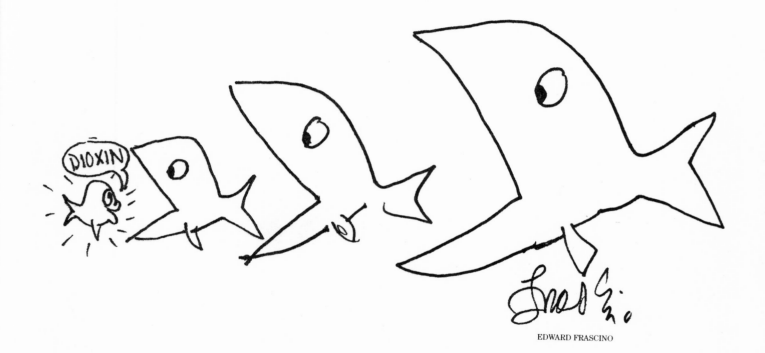

"This is my favorite spaghetti joint."

BUD GRACE

"We've got to stop taking our vitamins before dinner. I'm full."

BILL WOODMAN

INTRODUCING
THE PROVOLONE RANGER

MICHAEL CRAWFORD

"Is there any ketchup in the house?"

JACK ZIEGLER

© 1984 The New Yorker Magazine, Inc.

"For a more complete answer to that question, let us turn now to the *Book of Tofu*."

CATHERINE O'NEILL

"It's pasta primavera!"

PETER PORGES

BUD GRACE

S.GROSS

SAM GROSS

M.K. BROWN

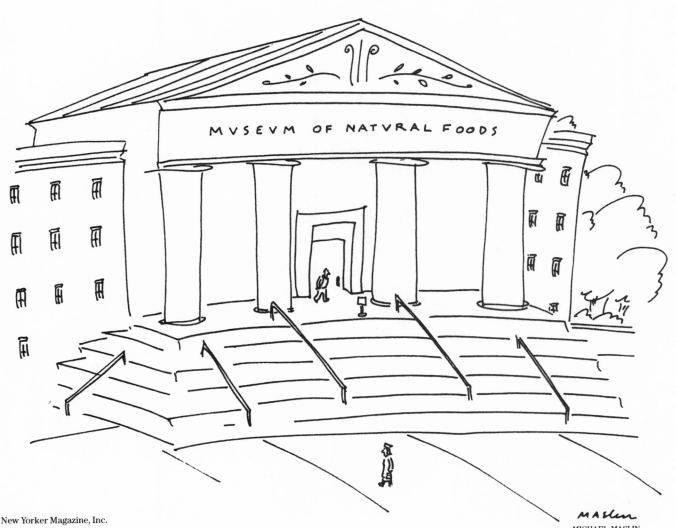

MVSEVM OF NATVRAL FOODS

MICHAEL MASLIN

EDWARD FRASCINO

"He claims I summoned him with my special blend of herbs and spices."

"I can't eat anymore, Fred, and I can't run anymore."

MORT GERBERG

No, no, I ordered pot au feu, not pot le fou!"

SAM GROSS

ROZ CHAST

AL ROSS

"Congratulations, you are now an educated wine
drinker. Congratulations, you are now an
educated wine drinker. Congratulations . . ."

ELDON DEDINI

"Remember, Marco, al dente on the noodles."

"Enzo writes that he's getting eighteen thousand lire for a plate of tagliatelle al formaggio on the lower East Side— and that's for *lunch!*"

DONALD REILLY

© 1986 The New Yorker Magazine, Inc.

"That may be Craig Claiborne. I asked him
to come over with his wok."

WARREN MILLER
© 1983 The New Yorker Magazine, Inc.

(continued) ➜

WOODMAN

BILL WOODMAN

"I'm sorry, sir, but our outdoor tables are reserved for
people who look French."

SIDNEY HARRIS

"Nutrition is very big these days. If anyone asks,
tell them that nutrition is your prime concern."

AARON BACALL

PHIL INTERLANDI

"Don't be alarmed. It's our first time in the non-smoking section."

CHILI   WITH A   10 SECOND DELAY

BERNARD SCHOENBAUM

JACK ZIEGLER

"What I want to know is when the hell 'petite'
became synonymous with 'nouvelle.'"

The Pita Puppets perform
" My Dinner with Andre."

OLIVER CHRISTIANSON (REVILO)

"Eat lots of fibre, drink plenty of fluids and be merry."

TIM HAGGERTY

"You ate it? That yogurt
was for my hair."

EDWARD FRASCINO

"This next piece is dedicated
to you carrots over there."

ELDON DEDINI

WOODMAN
BILL WOODMAN

"The one on the left is her personal nutritionist.

WARREN MILLER

"Thanks."

DAVID PASCAL

"Great stuff!"

LEO CULLUM
© 1985 The New Yorker Magazine, Inc.

"I've got the Los Angeles office on the line.
Does anyone need avocados?"

CRYSTO
PURE
SPRING
WATER
with Fiber

SWISS
THOMAS WUTHRICH (SWISS)

MANKOFF
ROBERT MANKOFF

"When it came to raisins, Mom's motto was "Use your imagination."

"Of course, I ate my vegetables . . .
I'm a vegetarian!"

WOODMAN

BILL WOODMAN

"Tell ya what, pal . . . let's just pretend I never heard you order those two wine coolers."

MARTY MURPHY

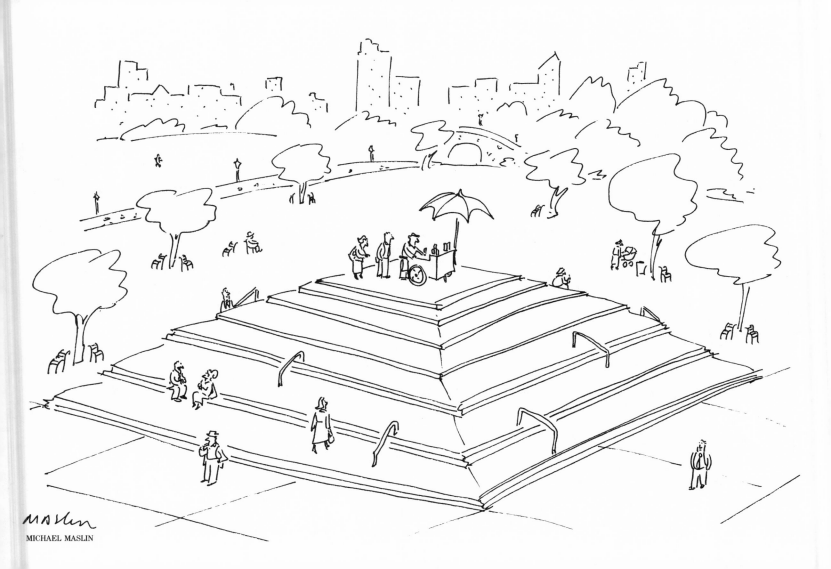

MICHAEL MASLIN

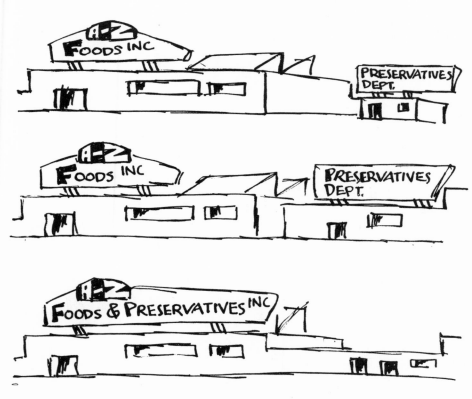

SIDNEY HARRIS

ELDON DEDINI

"I say it's designer food and to hell with it!"

S. GROSS

SAM GROSS

"Your car will be ready in about an hour. Would you care to try our salad bar?"

PETER STEINER

CHICKENS of the 'Eighties

Tennessee Tinies ~
The perfect size for the smaller, urban refrigerator.

1 Minute Wonders ~
These hens cook up so fast, they'll take your breath away.

Sportchickens ~
This new breed is all muscle and no fat.

New England Neverspoils ~
You can keep these pullets around for months - even years - at room temperature. They'll never go bad

R. Chast
ROZ CHAST

NURIT KARLIN

HENRY MARTIN

"...and eight tubs of vanilla. Vanilla
still seems to be the favorite."

TONY ROSA

SIDNEY HARRIS

"In nouvelle cuisine, we never explain and
we never apologize."

"The zucchini's in!"

ORLANDO BUSINO

"Oh, no! Not junk food!"

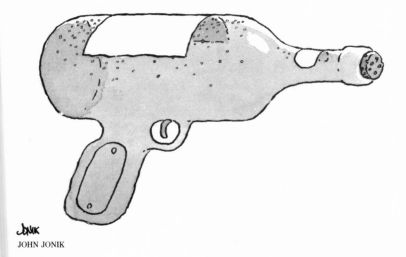

JOHN JONIK

EVOLUTION

MARINE COFFEE

DINOSAUR COFFEE

MR. COFFEE

Stuart Leeds
STUART LEEDS

"Here's your meatloaf, sir. In case of emergency, it can be used as a flotation device."

WILLIAM HOEST

MICHAEL MASLIN

"I'm at a secret training camp somewhere in the foothills of Connecticut. Behind me—
food and soft drink specialists, marching off to join the hamburger war."

L. TREPEL

AL ROSS

"I swear by Paul Newman's spaghetti sauce.
Now, if only Robert Redford made a pasta."

CLEM SCALSITTI

MICHAEL CRAWFORD

"These are roasted, oil and salt; these are roasted,
oil, no salt; these are dry roasted with salt;
these are dry roasted without; these are sun-dried
with salt; next are sun-dried without; and these
are fresh and raw with nothing."

WARREN MILLER

BRIAN SAVAGE

"Mrs. Ritterhouse had a dream last night. She dreamed about firm, fresh cucumbers, their skins uncoated with shelf-life-extending goop; tender zucchini and sweet corn; red, ripe, juicy tomatoes; big bunches of piquant basil; sprigs of herbs such as tarragon and sage. It's the same dream she had last year in February."

BOOTH
GEORGE BOOTH

JACK ZIEGLER

"Is that with or without goat cheese?"

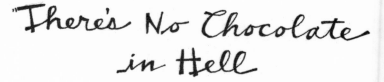

"There's No Chocolate in Hell

OLIVER CHRISTIANSON (REVILO)

EDWARD FRASCINO

"Hey, guys, I've put a twelve course dinner on the head of a pin."

THE END OF AN ERA: MAY 10, 1987:
Bean Sprouts Begin to Taste Weird

HEALTH HUT

ROZ CHAST

MICHAEL MASLIN

"Ed, I thought you cancelled Fruit-of-the-Month."

"Wow! Chocolate truffles. Can I have one?"

S.GROSS

SAM GROSS

HENRY MARTIN

"He was a man of simple tastes—
baked macaroni, steamed cabbage, wax beans,
boiled onions, and corn fritters."

MICK STEVENS

J. B. HANDELSMAN

"Miss, this seems to be blackened redfish.
We would have preferred reddened blackfish."

MOST ACTIVE BAGELS

SESAME	+⅞
GARLIC	−⅛
PLAIN	+¾
ONION	....
POPPY	−¼
PUMPERNICKEL	+½

STUART LEEDS

Sauers

CHARLES SAUERS

"I want the secret of your
barbecue sauce."

BILL WOODMAN

TIM HAGGERTY